An Ethnic Connection and Goals Beyond

Reflections of an Italian American Poet

second edition

Ron Iannone

Destination Press
Morgantown, West Virginia

© 2019 Ron Iannone

ISBN: 978-0-998-2020-4-4

An Ethnic Connection and Goals Beyond: Reflections of an Italian American Poet was originally published in 1975 and contained thirty-four of the poems presented here.

To Mary.

More than anybody else

you know why.

First Lines of Poems

I. An Ethnic Connection
    Late Sunday morn, I watched their promenade.................3
    On street corners 4
    I skimmed the local papers...5
    From city to city 6
    Between day and night...7
    For three decades I've spent my life
    suppressing its tenacity..11
    My albatross is fractionalization 12
    I think of what he said 13
    I struggle daily to understand my strangeness..................14
    I think 15
    Foreigners at our birth 16
    I feel tormented and overcome by what I've raised 17
    Sometimes starting with a howl 18
    All Sunday long friends and strangers
    alike came to her home 20
    Among strangers she was reticent.....................................21
    Above the sounds...22
    Oh yes! He was the man of the day..................................23
    In school, they told him to get rid of his accent 24
    So it goes on 25

II. And Goals Beyond
    I find myself with pen in hand...29
    The autumn's biting frost 31
    I talk, you listen..32
    In the dark...33
    Oh damn the confines of language...................................34
    Listen, my friend, I have found..35
    A celestial being found me 36
    In your simplicity 37
    The world gave birth to you..38
    I hear you talking outside my door 39
    Still I feel guilty 40
    In the day they passed as people in a crowd....................41
    Our lives are like the sea 44

Quickly!	45
I love almost uncontrollable speed	46
Sunsets and Sunrises	47
For me a Second	48
Your fingers were	49
Light Comes	50
There is nothing	51
Two ends of a continuum	52
Alone in church	53
We were two seeds	54
He said not	55
Time is	56
As a child, I don't	57
Driving Into New	58
At the End of Summer	59
Like that! Bam!	60
Wish we can	61
Looking through sheer curtains	62
There is a lull	63
I miss those Christmas Eves	64
In a dream, I'm	65
I love the darkness and	66
A few leaves	67
The landscape is always	68
Events don't	69
Light gray clouds	70
Leaves are moving then stationary, then	71
How much of my life	72
There is something	73
I lost myself	74
Even though I'm	75
Enjoyed Skaneateles	76
Today is gloomy	77
It is wonderful	78
Dreams	79
I would like	80
When I'm with	81
Thunder and hard	82
Everything is in full	83

Curved quarter	84
Up in Cortland, New York	85
Spring was	86
As I paint	87
Change is slow work	88
In small towns	89
Why is it now that I'm	90
She is a curvy	91
Sometimes I enjoy	92
Sidewalk blown	93
A wave of depression	94
I promise there	95
Each step I take	96
How many selves	97
I enjoy the	98
Someone once said	99
I feel the gathering	100
We know the	101
Everything seems better in the darkness	102
I hate it when	103
Winter is in the	104
We act like someone	105
If I was a bird	106
Sometimes when	107
When you stop	108
Fog lifting off	109
I fight the	110
The leaves have	111
The crisp cold of	112
The painting	113
Color is the	114
It's funny how you	115
Someone once said	116
A naked	117
Someone once said	118
I died last	119
I'm always	121
Everything seems better	122
That thing called	123

You know words	124
Most people look	125
You first bounce	126
Feel like an	127
I feel	128
When I stand before	129
I see the years	130

Preface

In 1975, I published my first collection of poems and reflections, *An Ethnic Connection and Goals Beyond.* Its pieces were largely grounded in my identity as an Italian American writer and in that which is beyond me.

Since that time, I've continued to observe my interior life and the world around me. As time has moved on, my notes, thoughts, reflections, and even songs, jotted down on index cards and steno pads, have become more free-form and concise. In 2017, in *Consequences,* I published another compilation of my work—a relatively small number of what had grown to my collection of some 2,000 brief pieces.

Here, I've updated *An Ethnic Connection and Goals Beyond,* keeping the original material largely as it was, but adding eighty-two poems to the second part of the book. My purpose in writing, and publishing, is to create short pieces that help readers get to their own feelings as they journey through life.

—Ron Iannone, 2019

I. An Ethnic Connection

Late Sunday morn, I watched their promenade,
Proudly and flamboyantly they strolled,
While above them an ubiquitous aroma floated about,
Then synchronized by her culinary preparations
I heard her beckoning me to come
Like a seagull calling its mate,
And when I arrived I found a table
Looking like a kaleidoscopic collage
Of pastels, reds and browns waiting for me,
And as epicures totally immersed and schooled
In their rites, we began in unison
Chewing, swishing and swirling to and fro,
So that from outside our apartment window
Our sounds were like the sea
Crashing against its innocent shores,

On this day we flirted
With the power of Machiavelli
And the uniqueness of da Vinci,
We were sculptors using space and air as our guides
Creating exquisite masterpieces by twisting
And gyrating pantomimes of Roman times,

Late in the afternoon exhausted
And satisfied from a day of fruitful labor,
A euphoric drowsiness lulled us to sleep
Somewhat similar to the surf
Curling about the toes of our feet,
Hell! We knew who we were
And our world was clearly defined,
Now we ask questions of identity
And what goals exist beyond.

———

On street corners,
And in front of stores,
They stand like birds
On splendid spring days,

Some think they were putting on a play,
But to them it was alive
To watch beautiful girls and virile men
Sauntering in grandeur about the street,

Sympathetic and compassionate to each other,
While jesting and joking
About subtle differences
Between girls' breasts and men's chests,

Questions were always the same,
Who is dying, what funeral passed,
And who is getting married
And laid,

When the sun faded, they left
Seeking adventurous and clandestine affairs,
For tomorrow they will try to outdo themselves
During the lulls in this watchful affair.

———

I skimmed the local papers
That sometimes caught up with me,
And a photo of a man
With tunnel-like eyes passed
In front of me,

I read
That he found tender pity
In a love affair
But I also read that an uncontrollable
Jealousy erupted against her other lover,
I guess he thought about
Another caressing her breast
And kissing her thighs,
So late one night silhouetted by the light
Of an escaping moon,
He hid behind a lilac bush
Like a predator waiting for his prey,

And thereafter spoiled the night's solitude
By firing a well-aimed shot
And with a huge anger in his heart
He shouted, "You son of bitch I'll show you."

A newly blacktopped driveway
Was sprinkled with a hue of red
And in spots looked like a Chinese checkerboard
Shit! I thought what intensity and audacity
It takes for him to still feel this way
In our age of coolness and opulence
And I think I almost envy his feat,
Now I know these are not proper American thoughts
But as a worn bloodstone loses its quartz
To the ravaging sea,
So too will this be lost amidst
The artifacts and events
Of the thousands of days that pass me by.

———

From city to city
The first thing I do
Is to go into their bookstores
Looking for poets who have
Last names ending in vowels,
Time after time I've found the Pounds, Eliots,
Frosts, Snyders, Blys, and others
Who obviously don't fit my criterion,
Yet one day in a bookstore in Boston
I came across two poets who have
Last names ending in vowels:
Nicki Giovanni and Lawrence Ferlinghetti,
So I searched through their biographies,
Oh how I prayed that they would fit my criterion,
What else can I say except that Nicki is black
And Lawrence is French.
But I still search among local bookstores
Hoping that a Del Santo, Mastroianni,
Rossi, Lo Castro, Pittarelli,
Calimeri and perhaps even an Iannone
Will turn up on the poetry shelf,
And then finally I might be able to understand my
Inner voice
A little bit
Better.

———

Between day and night
He searched for
A noon of his
Love life,

Like Don Quixote
The windmills
Thrust him up, up
To that dream above,

And a gentle sparkle
Was seen in his shadowed eyes
As the sun pierces the
Gray clouds on a stormy day

But inevitably
The windmills
Pushed him down, down
To that earth below,

Where
Some people
Thought him
Buffoon,

For there was a story
About the back seat
Of his 1948
Customized De Soto,

When he parked
On a desolate farm road
And in the process
Of denuding his prey,

Another car
Hurrying along at sixty
Collided
With their rear,
Hurling them forward
And whirling their bodies
Into the air
Like military missiles,

Later in the night a farmer
Found them
By the light
Of the moon,

Only donned
In clothes of
Bone marrow hue,
So it goes . . . on and on

Then there was the story
About the time
He strolled
Onto a beach,

Hopeful
All would recognize
A newly developed
Charles Atlas physique,

And as he took
Off his clothes
Somewhat
Discreetly,
Thunderous shouts

Of laughter, screams
Of shock and
Horrified faces of My God!

Broke the
Stillness
Of the
Calm sea air,

To this day
All remember
His cherry pink face
As he quickly stumbled away,

So much like a child
Running with his hands awkwardly
Covering those shameful parts,
So it goes . . . on and on.

Then there was a story
About a raucous affair
With a
Naughty lady,

Once they were
To meet in
A motel
That had questionable proclivities,

There he meticulously
Went over the sensuous stratagem
That
Would be,
And impatiently

He paced like a wolf
Sensing a female
In heat,
Until startled
By the sun
Refracting off
His window pane,

Somehow all was forgotten
In the passion
Of his anticipation,
So it goes . . . on and on.

For three decades I've spent my life suppressing its tenacity,
But it keeps gnawing like an unreachable difficulty,
Sometimes before I speak I feel it yowling and whining
Like another breath existing underneath mine,
And then it disrupts like an irascible and antagonistic child would
By shouts of
Listen to me!
"Youse guys,"
Listen to me!

———

My albatross is fractionalization
Soul mangled and twisted,
Gyrating into hyperbole!
Surrounded by fainting
Shouts of protests and wars!
And tantalized by songs
And rhetoric of messages,

My sea echoes
Truths are tenable!
Traditions are vanishing!
Relationships are temporary!
Loves are sensual!

My eunuch is the sea!
Knowing an avenging deity
Lurks in its watery spray!
To fall upon pebbles
Reflecting my destinies!

I think of what he said,
Of fiery sunsets;
Of stewing seas;
Of soft flurries of snow;
Of amber flames dancing about;
"All must suffer, sacrifice
And die,"
But it is I
I am the celebrant
But I know he'll say,
"I wish I talked
To that boy more."

———

I struggle daily to understand my strangeness
And to keep myself from anonymity
And only while listening to the sounds
Beneath subtle murmurs of the sea,
Do I hear someone playing a song for me.

———

I think
I am what
I
see,

I think
I am what
I
hear,

I think
I am what
I
feel,

I think
I am what
I
taste,

I think
I am what
I
touch,

I think my soliloquy
Is simple—
Unlike what
I think I am.

Foreigners at our birth,
A womb replaced by insecurities,
An umbilicus replaced by uncertainties,
A placenta replaced by artificialities,

Contradictions of our
Inhabitance are elicited,
Illuminating human fears, hates, and loves
Exonerated! Exorcised!

Yet fertilized with
Incipient strangeness,
This now becomes
Our embryo!

I feel tormented and overcome by what I've raised,
To explode without warning at the slightest clamor,
And then to unleash the violence of the wild sea,
Also to be intolerant of rivals in both love and worldly affairs,
And then to strike them with the weaponry of verbality,
It is like counting the beads on the rosary I ask why each time
Seeking answers I know will never be.

———

Sometimes starting with a howl,
"Plunk your magic twanger, Froggie."
I journeyed
On an evening star,

With one twist
A visceral
Odyssey would
Begin,

Still other times
Histrionics and epigrams abounded,
Anti-intellectual and banal yes,
But ever so comforting,

And when stars
In the sky
Were diamonds
On velvet,

An ecstatic
Voice
Shouted "It's
Goin', Goin', Gone,"

For a moment and similar
To the first spring flower,
Fame and brightness
Became all mine,

Yet before I knew
What was happening
A cocoon was spun
By thousands of electronic dots,
So few things

Were left
With logical consequences
And truths being absolute,

Until the electronic dots
Massaged and danced over me
Then all was
Fine,

I think I said enough
Of this, except maybe,
I lost something like
A train passing in the night.

———

All Sunday long friends and strangers alike came to her home
Searching for something comforting,
Like a strong summer breeze skews the water
From a marble cherub fountain
So it was for her,
Droplets of Love and Joy fell on everyone
That came near,
And when her husband died
She was to lament for a while
But her love of humanity lingered on,
And like a candle burns from the inside
And spills over
Until nothing,
Then eternity!
So it was for her.

Among strangers she was reticent
But her luminous eyes were always present,
And one felt somehow she was Plato or Kant
Pondering a contradiction,

But the source of her sinews took place
Before dawn
In the preparations
Of culinary celebrations,
So that with the zeal and passion,
Of a fiery priest
She brought this into fruition,
And like the consecration in Mass
The substance of her family
Was mystically transformed
Into the unity of one.

———

Above the sounds,
Of scissors clipping and men conversing
A light concerto could be heard,
Against this background he performed with strength and harmony
And when kindled by the heart
He fought even harder for human dignity,
But as he got older
The sounds faded with the wind,
So that he was left alone with only an eternal dream,
That of a far-off soil which might contain
A potential for birth and immortality.

———

Oh yes! He was the man of the day,
Women and athletics were always his affair,
All of his world seemed to be in these,
Juxtaposed with Pride and Passion he journeyed afar,

Unexpectedly his journey passed into darkness,
As time became his greatest foe,
He found fertile ground for only one seed,
While his masculinity and all the rest went astray,

He frantically searched
In loins of whores
And alcoholic stupors
To no avail,

In desperation he hoped to rejuvenate himself
By looking to the sea,
But there he only found reflections
Of his fears and vacuities,

Near the end his friends tried to help
But because of his way this didn't work,
It was like having premonitions of a friend's death
Then feeling powerless in its presence.

In school, they told him to get rid of his accent
Sound out his missing "th's" and round out his "ing,"
At sixteen he guarded the door at the state house,
Before leaving for work each day
His parents told him he must be a "nicea boy,"
So he would be always employed,

One day his bosses said when he spoke to those above him:
"He must speak with hat in hand."
This, they said, was because he was not really in his land,
They said this city was settled by the best,
And he must remember he would always be less,
They told him never to outwardly show affection
For in this city, one had to walk with sophistication,

On his twentieth birthday he decided to stay home
And for the next forty years this is where he remained.
Nobody really understood why he seemed to be in pain,
On a clear brisk fall day, they found him
In the grotto with a bullet in his head,
On his face were signs of anguish and dread,
Tightly clutched in hand was a note
Written on an old bread wrapper,
All that could be understood were the words,
"I am Wop so Whatsamatter."

———

So it goes on,
On and on
Wondering why
I do the things I do,

That I revere
The softness
Of life
Amidst its madness,

That I learn
From poets
Of humanity
And its frailties,

That I know
Soldiers have wars
Politicians have scandals
And I have apathy,

That I struggle
To identify the contradictions
Of civilization
Within me,

That I ask
Myself what is
Beyond all
Of this,

That I find
No answers except perhaps
In a fleeting moment
Of a sun-filled day.

———

II. AND GOALS BEYOND

I find myself with pen in hand
Unable to describe what occurs
Daily in front of me,
I know the idylls of
Dylan Thomas would be proper,
Yet I feel what occurs
In front of me is almost
Too emotional, too aesthetic, too mystifying
For conventional description,

And as I gain an understanding
Of what occurs in front of me,
Other mysteries are elicited
Like links of a chain leading me
To the understandings
And order of things,
But each link becomes more arduous
Than the previous,
So now I have accepted the reality
That I will never bring totality to these things,

But I do find a degree
Of satisfaction in daily listing these:
There are the seagulls staging
Their human conditions for me;
There is the juxtaposition
Of planes soaring over urbanity,
Of seagulls in flight,
Of clamdiggers racing the tides;
It is like gazing at the paradoxes of humanity,

And then there are the loons
And other divers alike
Challenging me with their agility;
And there are the far-off

Islands of abiding mystery
Whose names and beginnings
I know reek with history
And looking beyond their biographies,
Beyond their forts that now stand empty,
Beyond their soldierless parade grounds,
Beyond the ghostly sounds of the drummers' roll,
Beyond all of this
I think about what William Faulkner said,
"Listen my stranger, this is myself, this is I."

The autumn's biting frost
And its facades of nakedness has
Chased them away
And once they are gone,
The days become brighter
And the sun glistens again,

And no longer do you
Worry about them
Spoiling the
Whiteness and purity of your skin,
For I know in retrieving yourself
You are really
Cleansing yourself
Of the despair
They left behind,

My God! You can be profane and
Stubborn in your fury but also
Somber and compassionate in your calm
And it is because of this
That I walk softly and reverently
Along your smooth borders
For I don't want to miss your words
Found in my thoughts,
Now it is only the gulls,
You and I remaining,
And together we walk
In peace,
Seeking to understand
The fuzzy truths
Of the universe.

I talk, you listen,
You talk, I listen,
I talk, you listen—Oh God!
The never-ending cyclical
Dialogue, strangers, friends,
Lovers find no solace in this;
It is so meaningless, passionless,
Expressionless and ever so frustrating.

I talk, you listen, you talk
I listen, frantically hoping
It will be different
That I will find camaraderie,
Love and brotherhood,
I search in vain among friends,
Lovers and strangers
All I find is loneliness,
Despair and fear.

I talk, I talk, I talk!
———————

In the dark
Of the night
Often you spoke
Of unknown fears,

And when dawn appeared
Our eyes would meet
By the light
Of the morn,

And all my problems
With you were forgotten
As we softly and gently
Touched each other,
Like the discreet
Winds of summer.

Oh damn the confines of language,
Our tongues cannot express
Our struggles and contradictions,

Our hearts cannot express
Our love for humanity
Without the superficiality of words,

In our solitude and in our quest for truth
We are caught
In an empty web of terms and symbols,

But just for a moment,
A flash of a moment, the ironies
Of our despairs are the radii of our growth

And our beings just for a moment,
A flash of a moment are brought closer
To the center of humanity.

———

Listen, my friend, I have found
An island of tranquility and serenity,
Inhabitants with faces of British Gentry.
And the stubbornness of Prometheus,

Listen, my friend, I have found
Some unscarred and ubiquitous hills,
Their bowels clothed by virgin oak, poplar and birch,
Deciduous pantheon of laurels, marigolds and rhododendrons.

Listen, my friend, I have found
The religious fervor of Kierkegaard,
The sensitivity of James Joyce,
And the reverence of William Faulkner.

Listen, my friend, I have found
Faces scarred by coal, money, and power,
Yet don't despair my friend,
Their eyes search for friends, not pity.

Listen my friend, I have found
At last! A moment of quietude,
That insulates me
From the clamor of worldly noises.

———

A celestial being found me,
Athena I thought or a sculpture to be gazed at,
Long Roman black hair hugged a vest
And sensuous eyes and watery lips tempted me,
I dreamed we were in a meadow covered
With heavenly dew,
And there we played, touched and danced
To the tunes of God's chosen few,
As I spoke in generalizations
You spoke with the softness of carnal delight,
And all the while we were soaring higher into paradise
Until the domino dotted sky faded behind Gotham
As it illuminated its night,
And there I lost her
To the Gods guiding our flight.

In your simplicity
You have given me reality
In your ruralness
You have given me individuality,

In your compassion
You have given me hope,
In your perceptibility
You have given me vision,

Bound not by proper contract,
But by a bondage of mirrors
In you I am,
And in me you are,

And you too are my womb
Lying with you by the open fire,
Making love to you on Sunday afternoon,
Walking with you near the sea,

Before I met you
I thought love was too elusive
And only existed in the minds
Of Hallmark card writers,

Now I think I know
What love is
And how it follows
The laws of the flowers.

———

The world gave birth to you
On a special day in May,
Since then three tens and more have passed
And the world seems to be in a disarray,
To this condition, "Let's have a good time."
You've been known to say,

Majestically, your huge
Green eyes give away your
Childlike innocence,
For you, people come first,
To listen and to give
Will always be your special way,

Strangers can't believe you're
For real in this dangerous age,
But like the healing powers
Of a flowering sage
You have helped us all
To be more humane.

———

I hear you talking outside my door
I hope you'll let me share my soul
And listen to me with compassionate concern,
"I know you're there. Come in!"

I hear you talking outside my door
I hope you'll change my loneliness
And change my fate,
"I thought you would never come,"

I hear you talking outside my door
I hope you'll drink with me from the chalice of uncertainties
And we'll talk about truths in tiny things,
"Stop ducking out of sight,"

I hear you talking outside my door
I hope you'll be the midwife of spring
And all its eternal meanings,
"I want to cry,"

I hear you talking outside my door
I hope you'll be like a spirited seagull
And together we'll fly off into cloud-blown skies,
"I wish you wouldn't giggle in the hallway,"

"Oh God! Stop peeking in at me."

———

Still I feel guilty
For searching
For something
That only fame brings

Still to solicit
Love
Of strangers
Frustrates me,

Still this obsession
With fame
Puzzles
Me,

Still
Irregular
Poems
Flow,

Still poets
Of the universe
Say
"Be patient,"

Still poets
Like myself are
Born in
An age of immediacy,

Still . . .
What is it
All
For?

In the day they passed as people in a crowd
But in the dark of the night their noises were apparitions for me,
I heard her shuffle across the floor below,
I heard his strange noises in the bathroom next to me,
Now and then I also heard a girl giggle above,
Like a voyeur I developed in time
An acumen for visual imagery;

One evening the widow who boarded me
Spoke in tones that her grayish complexion implied,
She said she would be away for ten days,

On the night following her departure
I examined her memorabilia scattered about
As I've previously done with the discerning
Carvings on a sycamore tree,
Yet this is not all, for while I was
Engaged in this activity,
I heard different noises;
I heard the weathered house crack and clamor;
I heard the dull humming of the grandfather clock;
I heard children's voices outside ebbing away;
I heard the weird stillness of a house unoccupied,
Then Oh God then I heard eerie deathlike sounds
Of rhythmically heavy breathing
Crescendoing into the heavens above,
For a moment time and eternity became one
Like a sentry I listened and directed my attention
To the source of the sounds,

It seemed to be coming from her battered mahogany desk,
And when I opened the top drawer
An acrid odor of a freshly smoked pipe hit my nostrils
I wished my mother was here for I recalled my fear
I had as a child,

When I would go into the cellar for homemade goods
Always thinking that someone else was there,
And I would run up the cellar stairs taking
Them two at a time
Never looking back for fear that someone was behind,

Soon afterwards everything seemed to fade
Into the quiet of the night
So I continued to work until midnight,
Then I went upstairs to my ten by ten room
And its crazy wallpaper design
Of tiny yellow droplets infused
With a myriad of silvered five point stars,
Oh how insane this room was,
Now when I closed the door behind me
The eerie sounds started again
With even more intensity than before
Like an angel having a cardiac attack,

All I could recall is that
The next moment became frozen in time
Like a frame in a 16mm film,
I saw myself in another room
Watching the play of the moon,
While it illuminated a decor of white satin and ruffles
And silhouetted objects of different hue,
Then I can't explain why but I spoke
To the sounds,
I almost panicked when
I felt a peaceful calm take hold of me,
At the time I thought what a crazy response
And before I could comprehend the totality of the moment

I was dreaming of tender mysteries,
I was never to hear the sounds again
Except one brisk wintry night at two in the morn,
I found her sitting in the living room
With all the lights aglow,
There she sat not noticing me
Staring into a light directly above,
As before I felt the same peaceful calm
But now I felt the respect one feels
Towards a person praying reverently,

At noon the next day she passed
My open door in what seemed a troubled way,
So I asked about her condition
Incoherently she spoke about never becoming a victim
Of a long illness as he,
And she had hidden a bottle of pills
That would eliminate this possibility,

Soon after this I left
And I had suppressed these happenings
To the abysmal depths of my dreams
But yesterday I remembered all
When I read in the daily obituaries
"Mrs. _____ . . . died Friday
After a short illness . . .."

Our lives are like the sea,
Its surface distorts
Its innermost depths,
And so with us
Our lives become a lie
And our souls hide
In the shadows
Of our tomorrows.
———

Quickly!
Quickly!
Fast!
Fast!
Done!
She says
I'm
Rushing
To Death
And So
It
Goes!

———

I love almost uncontrollable speed
In Boats and Convertibles
Because it
Brings you
Close to Death
You can almost
Touch It,
Then Quickly
You Escape,
Sometimes, Sometimes,
It Almost Tears
Your Face Off
With Cheeks
Bubbling
Only the Sting
Can be Felt,
Yes, it's
Scary But
Something
Tells you you can beat
It, As if you jump
Off a Cliff and Survive the
Rocky Shore below.

———

Sunsets and Sunrises
Are Explosions
Of Colors; Reds,
Purples, Pinks,
Yellows,
I'm in awe when
I experience them,
Time after Time.

———

For me a Second
Generation Italian
American,
There was a definite
Distinction Between
Us and Them,
For instance we had the
Bread Man,
Ice Man, Fruit Man,
Vegetable Man,
Watermelon Man,
We would wait for
Their Calls, Their
Yells, Their
Individual Distinctive
Sound, It was
So part of us,
Later on
I Realized they
Made us so
Different.

Your fingers were
Long and Strong
Like the great
Violinist Itzhak
Perlman,
But now your
Wings pointed
In all directions
As conducting
Your last symphony,
Along with whispering to me,
"Let me go this is
No way to live,
I lived as long
And good as I could,
Let me go, please."
28 hours later
He was gone,
I was also gone,
Thinking there was
More Time,
You see I wanted
You to know
That I always
Wanted to please you,
But even in death
You made me feel
Guilty again because
I left when you
Passed
Without seeing you conduct
Your last song.

———————

Light Comes
Through the
Window and
It Gives a Different
Image of the
Girl and Boy
I painted Standing Under
The White
Umbrella.

———

There is nothing
For you to say to me
Anymore,
I held your emaciated
Hand as life
Left you,
I thought you
Squeezed mine
Affectionately
But I'm not sure
You never liked
To be touched
Except you loved
To touch the
Hair of your
Caregivers, All Women—in fact,
I was jealous
But understood,
For now you
Have become silent,
They took you away,
Tightly wrapped from head to toe in
A White Sheet,
Quickly they rolled
You by me
As if they didn't
Want me to notice
It was you,
That's not right,
So sad, in these
Places they take
Your dignity away
Now I wish I
Could see you
Again, One last time,
To say
Mom, I love you.

Two ends of a continuum
Of Reality
The abstract and the real,
Most important is
The in-betweenness
And how to survive
The twilight is the
Most difficult
Phase of life.

Alone in church
I look at the flickering
Of vigil lights on the ceilings,
Walls, statues, etc.,
I saw the statues
Moving,
I sat down in a pew
To pray but really
It was an excuse
So I can just
Rest from the
Outside turmoil
And Chaos.

———

We were two seeds
Blown together into flight
By the breezes of humanity,
Gently coming to rest
Upon each other in a
Field of celestial bliss.
Then, however, we are
Jolted into the heavens
By the raging wind
And throwing us askew
Every which way,
Mindfully aware that
Our flight now will
Be alone without you
Until I feel the
Silent nudges of your
Love saying I am
Still here.

———

He said not
To enjoy
Too Much
Because the bad
Will quickly follow,
And I will lose
The ability to
Create Ideas,
Forget fame and money he said
For it takes
Away the Pain you
Need to write
Good thoughts
And Stories.

———

Time is
In Me
Sometimes
Is Lost
In between
Yesterday,
Today,
And Tomorrow,
It Flows
Like a River
Infusing over
Every Word
And Gesture,
I'm aware
Of It
When I lie awake
With Insomnia
Looking at the
Numbers flipping
By on the
Digital Clock
Everything around
Me is
Expiring.

———

As a child, I don't
remember ever
telling my mother
my favorite things,
I never went
to her room because
of a nightmare.
I always
felt sad for the
person I was,
She never comforted
Me, She never
told me she loved
me, and I never
assumed she did,
She did what society expected
of mothers.
Oh, yes, and
one time she
bought me a
toy train set called,
American Flyer!

———

Driving Into New
York I see
The Silver Buildings
That look like
The tips of Silver
Swords,
Once out of the Taxi
I felt a Burst of
Energy and Excitement
That almost
Takes My
Breath Away.
———

At the End of Summer
I saw a small
Patch of Intense
Red Color Peeking
Through the
Dull Green Leaves.
———

Like that! Bam!
Green, Everything is beautifully Green!
Ugliness is Gone
And Beauty Wins
For a While.

Wish we can
be sitting on the
beach drinking
wine and
listening to the
steady beat
of the waves
over and over
and then
going to another
dimension where
you can be
you and I can
be me and we
fly, fly.

―――――――

Looking through sheer curtains
Streetlights look like
The blinking and guiding star that
Is usually in pictures at Christmastime,
Then as I move further back
Some of them look like
Flying saucers through
The reflection of the window.
———

There is a lull
In the winter when everything
Seems to have stopped growing,
All time and life for a while gets a reprieve
Then it springs back.

———

I miss those Christmas Eves
A word of God describes them best,
The word Glory, that was it! I know now!
Glory, they were all of that! And More!
I think about the sweet sounds
Of my Uncles and Aunts talking and laughing,
Enhancing what we were
By their intensity,
And rich hearts!
I think about the eels and snails
They cooked,
Too pungent for me, but
Combined with tomato sauce—
An edible delight,
At such times, they would always plead,
"Mange [eat], now Mange!"
When these words were spoken,
I felt
Love and warmth,
We were
Like seeds that grew
By plan and design
For many years to come—
To fire the human spirit!

———

In a dream, I'm
Walking along in a
Dark corridor when
I find a door that opens
To a garden of hope,
I find a higher
Level of paradise there,
Then suddenly the inevitable happens
Melancholy and despair
Catches up with me.

———

I love the darkness and
Peace of early morn
It seems it's just
me and
Nature,
I own the world.
———

A few leaves
moving and I
try to remain still,
Let nature lead
me to calmness.
───────

The landscape is always
here and I
haven't anywhere
near exhausted
my wonder of
It.
———

Events don't
move fast enough
for me. I want them
to happen so
I can move on to
the next and
finally rest and
Say see all I
accomplished
today.

———

Light gray clouds
and rain feeds the
depression, stuckness,
Need to move beyond
Ghosts from
Everywhere.
———

Leaves are moving then stationary, then drifting, then stationary . . . what's coming? What surprises does nature have for us today? So everything is changing. You never know when it's going to be calm, fickle, intense or explosive. I love people like that too. Society calls them crazy, I call them interesting.

———

How much of my life
I have faked it,
pretended it,
Is there anything
I do truly genuine
Or is It all
False?
———

There is something
in me that likes
working with earth
and doing really
hard work so
I work up a
sweat.
Afterwards I
ache but feel good
that I can see
what I accomplished
As also with painting.
Writing is something else,
you never know
whether people
see what you see.

———

I lost myself
in my painting
again. Centered
on painting and
nothing else.
Let the paint
lead me.
That is what Mary
Richards talks about
in Centering. Lose
yourself in another
Realm.

———

Even though I'm
in this world
I feel I'm outside,
As people
and family talk
I only half hear as I really
Listen to other
Thoughts that exist
In other realms.

Enjoyed Skaneateles
Lake and its
cool breeze and
smell of its
fish in water.
Also Anyela's
winery was great.
Had too much
wine and slept
for the rest of the
day.
———

Today is gloomy,
I see no birds
flying and it
seems the flowers
are taking a rest
from blooming.

———

It is wonderful
Being in Love
You always want
To be with
That person
and carry
That person
With You.
It seems you
Can't function
Without hearing
Or seeing that
Person Living or
Being with you
Every minute
Of every Day.
Sounds so
Corny, but that's
The meaning of Love.
———————

Dreams
are like stars
you can't really
ever reach but
can lead us to our
new destiny.
———

I would like
to experience pure
bliss and
become one
with nature.
———

When I'm with
nature, I feel
everything is
right with the
world.
———

Thunder and hard
Like rain makes
Home a cozy
Blanket for me
That I want to
Cuddle with.

―――――

Everything is in full
bloom especially
the lilacs. I love
the sweet
smell. It's
Like a flower
Of love.
———————

Curved quarter
moon,
I see an
older man looking
Down on me and
Giving me strength.
―――――

Up in Cortland, New York
I always enjoy the
Simplistic life
There.
I don't have
to be on,
I don't have to be the show,
Just me.
———

Spring was
full out this morning
with the new
blossoms and dogwoods
and crab apples.
Color was overflowing.
———

As I paint
an image of a barn,
my mind wants
the colors to
Take me over.
———

Change is slow work.
It is not for neither the
faint-hearted nor the
impatient.
———

In small towns
it's all sameness
and every day
nothing significant
is happening.
I notice the
beautiful people are missing in
small town happenings.
Everyone just looks simple,
plain and boring.
I love having
beautiful people
around like
I had in the
theatre world.
Beautiful people
are vanishing in our
society. Where
are the interesting
people too?
Cyber world
sucks these people
away. We
fake becoming
interesting and
falsifying beauty with
working out and
all that stuff.
The natural beauty
seems to be good.
As we wear
masks of beauty,
Like we all are in one large
Cosmic movie.

———

Why is it now that I'm
finishing paintings
in less than an
hour and I'm
usually happy
with it. That is
not true with
my writing. Over
and over, I go over
the sentences until
I feel it's my voice,
Finally, I get
rid of all the
other voices
even though I have
learned from them.
———————

She is a curvy
woman with red
hair and freckles
that I met at
a neighborhood
car wash.
She had Big
Blue eyes, high
cheekbones framing
a small triangle
of a nose.
Full lips that
turned slightly
downward at the
Corners.

Sometimes I enjoy
doing errands
so I don't have
to think about
the seriousness of
Life and Death.
Think Nothing!
Rest from
Worries and
Pain.
Where are the
Angels in my Life,
Taking away the
Demons?

———

Sidewalk blown
over with sand,
They took it all in,
the gulls and the
waves, the bikini
clad girls, the boys
in board shorts, the
lifeguard in his
wooden tower, young
people so black
they should have
been making commercials
for tanning beds,
Some
played volleyball
with no one watching.
Some ran with
their dogs.
Some lay
out on brightly
patterned towels
the size of bed
sheets.

———

A wave of depression
hits early, then
love from others
brings sunshine
into my life.
———

I promise there
always will be a
little place
no one will ever
see,
A tiny part
deep in my heart
that stays in
Love with you.
_____

Each step I take
Scientists say
Destroys a little
Bit of my
Living Cells
Until They
Are all
Gone and
Death Is the
Final Result,
It's kind of
Suicide for
Humanity.
———

How many selves
do I have?
The shy and quiet
person and non-confident,
The forward confident,
outgoing person,
I feel more comfortable
with the shy,
unsure and
not having a lot of
people around,
As I get older the
quiet and shy
is winning out.

———————

I enjoy the
deep dark of
early mornings
and late at
night.
———

Someone once said
It's not the years
in your life that
count . . .. It's the
life in your years.
———————

I feel the gathering,
darkening
of lust that follows
me all the time
threatening to burst.
―――――

We know the
fantasy or dream
is always better
than reality.
———

Everything seems better in the darkness
than in lightness,
Night offers more
in its shadows
Than in sunlight.
That's why
Our Stories, Poems,
And Movies Do
Best in Darkness.

―――――

I hate it when
people try to
be someone they're
not or play
games with
relationships. They
want to be chased
or Hunted as
Hemingway says.

Winter is in the
air with colder
days and frost
at night. Mums
still perk up during
sunny fall days.
Leaves are changing
fast and falling.
I look forward
to the first snow
flakes.

———

We act like someone we're not. It's often because we're not happy who we are. We think we need other people's permission or love or approval before we can live our lives and pursue who we are.

———

If I was a bird
I would see
everything, The whole
world. But from
far away, like a
blurry painting.
One of those that
looks beautiful
and simple until
you got close
enough to see
the imperfections.

———

Sometimes when we ask God for an answer, He sends us a friend. Figure out who He's already sent to you.

———

When you stop learning, your mind stops expanding. If I don't have a worry every day, I find it difficult to get through. Once a worry is created and taken care of, I create another one. For me, once a worry is resolved, another pops into my mind to replace it. I think this is what makes me unique. Part of who I am. I need worries as nourishment to grow as a unique individual.

Fog lifting off
the lake as
a curtain going
up and
showing the spectacular
colors of summer
with a deep
green-bluish lake
dominating.

―――――

I fight the
idea to take
Painting lessons
So I can paint
Like everyone
Else. No!
I paint like I
want to and have
My own style
Of Color helping
Who I am.
I don't want
To paint what
Your find in a glossy
Photo.
It's staying
In the Lines
Versus my Abstract
Realism or outside the
Line paintings.

The leaves have
Lost their yellow
Luster before they
Blow away,
They'll
Come back again
Next Fall with
Their intense Colors
Like civilizations
That decay and then are reborn,
Repeated
Over and Over.

The crisp cold of
mornings, the partial
remaining leaves
on the trees,
soon the
first flakes will
Be here.
———

The painting
Took off in a different
Direction than
I planned. It
seems now to
represent two
people walking
Through a dark
Forest and ahead is
A beautiful lake
High up Between
Two mountains.
Something you
May see in Heaven.

Color is the
Way I'm going
In Painting. I'm
totally surprised
by What I want
to do.
Images pop
Through in
The Abstractness.

———

It's funny how you
can be in a room
full of people and
still feel alone.
———

Someone once said
that thinking about
someone often enough
will make them
appear. They will be
in your thoughts and then suddenly
they will be standing
behind you at the
grocery store or
in the car next
to you at a
traffic light,
It happens all the
Time to me.
It's, I think, my guardian
Angel speaking to me
It blows my Mind!
When you've
gone years
without seeing
them at all.

———

A naked
Soul
Looks
For an
Anchor
To
Guide
Its
Beliefs.
———

Someone once said,
"We always center more
on our scars than
our healing."
———

I died last
night and came
back from the
edge of the
other world. I
felt pain and
couldn't move
as something was
pulling me
Through a tunnel.
I was still conscious
of a lighted bedroom
with a TV on. I
tried calling
my wife
for help but
nothing comes
out. My legs,
arms were
all frozen. I
said to myself I
wasn't ready
to go and fought
to gain control
and eventually I
felt movement
coming back to
my limbs. Lastly
I was able to gain
my voice back with
slurred speech
at first. The next
time I worry it
may be for good
leaving this

world and
finding out what
is the other
end of the tunnel.
———

I'm always
surprised at what
results when I
paint. I think
muted dark
grays and blacks
But I end up
with yellows,
purples,
reds, and
blues
I see things
nobody else sees.
I see in my head
but not as
others see
in reality. This
is my style to
let the bright colors go like
A jazz musician
that comes back
every once in
a while to a few
standard chords.

Everything seems better
when we were younger,
Our lives, spring, sun,
moon, girls, ideas,
Now today everything
Seems muted, dull,
and gray,
Not like it was yesterday.
―――――

That thing called
Age creeps in
Morning Walks,
Confusion in mind,
Muscles don't
Follow what
The mind wants
To do.
I didn't see her in
The picture,
Later in the
Day, I thought
It's my wife
I think,
However, I still need
to accomplish
Something each
Day. Purpose
Is needed Or
Death begins to
Creep In.

You know words
Can't really describe
How much you
Mean to me,
Even though you're
Only 3 feet tall
And somewhat small
I'm blessed to have
You as my best friend
For all of mine are gone now.
I love you for
You don't
Conform like others,
When we play
Your eyes sparkle
Like stars in the sky,
Your love is
Unconditional
And forever,
Our time together
Will soon end
So goodbye and
Take care, my friend.

———

Most people look
At me and think
He's got everything,
Fame and Money,
How can he be
Depressed,
But they don't know
When they say
I love the music
You brought us,
You see I don't
Believe them,
So I ignore them
And keep sailing on,
I love the praise
But I hate it
Because I know
It will go away soon.

You first bounce
to life, then
sprint, then
crawl and finally
stop in its
face. Death.
———

Feel like an
empty glass
today. Tired
and no juice
to move
I need a boost.
———

I feel
My Memory
Vanishing
Daily,
I'm
Tired of Trying
To remember
Names
And
Places.
———

When I stand before
God at the end of
my life, I would
hope that I would
not have a single
bit of talent left
so I could say
I used everything
You gave me.

––––––––

I see the years
Passing me
Everything is going
Faster,
Changes are here
And gone Tomorrow
I look for Comfort
As I'm running Scared,
Seeking someone
To take my hand
And hold me.

———

About the Author

Ron Iannone has degrees from St. Bonaventure University and University of Rochester as well as having attained his doctorate from Syracuse University, with post-graduate work at Harvard. He has written a number of books, articles, plays, and screenplays, with a particular focus on education. His books are known nationally, especially *School Ain't No Way: Appalachian Consciousness*, which has been re-issued. His other recent publications include *Consequences: Short Stories, Poems, Commentaries*; a compilation of plays and screenplays, *Voices on the Edge*; and the novels *A Boston Homecoming* and *A Not So Normal Family*. He is also the founder of West Virginia Public Theatre.

He has received two lifetime achievement awards for his contributions as a writer, educator, poet, and artist, and as an outstanding Italian American in West Virginia. In 2015, he received West Virginia University's College of Human Services Hall of Fame award.

www.ingramcontent.com/pod-product-compliance
Lightning Source LLC
Chambersburg PA
CBHW032135040426
42449CB00005B/258